ANIMAL PREY

Porcupines

SANDRA MARKLE

⌐ LERNER PUBLICATIONS COMPANY / MINNEAPOLIS

THE ANIMAL WORLD
IS FULL OF
PREY.

Prey are the animals that predators eat. Predators must find, catch, kill, and eat other animals in order to survive. But prey animals aren't always easy to catch or kill. Some have eyes on the sides of their heads to let them see predators coming from all directions. Some are colored to blend in and hide. Some prey are built to run, leap, fly, or swim fast to get away. And still others sting, bite, or use chemicals to keep predators away. *Porcupines all over the world have built-in weapons—special hairs that are stiff, needlelike quills.*

There are two families of porcupines. Old World porcupines live in Africa, Asia, India, and parts of Europe. The Old World group, like these crested porcupines, mainly live and eat on the ground.

New World porcupines live in South and Central America, most of the United States (except the Southeast), and in Canada. New World porcupines, like this North American porcupine, spend much of their time in trees.

It's late August in a northern forest in the United States, the home of this male North American. The porcupine has slept all day in an oak tree. As it gets dark, he climbs down and waddles off in search of one of his favorite feeding trees. Along the way, he smells ripe berries and follows his nose to this treat. The big male is about the size of a sturdy, medium-sized dog. He is armored with sharp quills, so he has few enemies. Still, he stays alert for predators as he lingers on the ground nibbling his berry snack.

The male porcupine moves on to a pine tree where he's fed before. He digs his long, curved nails into cracks in the tree bark and starts to climb. The bumpy skin on the soles of his feet keeps him from slipping. His tail, covered in stiff bristles, helps too. The porcupine climbs until he can reach the tree's slender, tender branches. He nips off a branch with his big, chisel-shaped front teeth. These teeth have an extra-sturdy enamel coating on the outer surface. The coating makes the animal's teeth strong enough to bite through wood. Gnawing branches and bark wears down his front teeth, so they keep on growing.

A noise makes the porcupine look down. He spots a young mountain lion climbing toward him. A big cat will take on a porcupine when other prey is scarce. A cat that is young and inexperienced like this one doesn't know better. The porcupine chatters by clicking his teeth together. As a further warning to the big cat to leave him alone, he squawks loudly. But the young mountain lion keeps on climbing up the tree.

The porcupine prepares to defend himself. He presses his quill-free belly against the tree trunk. The quills on his back, buried under his long guard hairs, become erect. It is a reaction similar to the one that makes people have goose bumps. This way, he is armed with more than thirty thousand quills. They fan out in every direction, from his cheeks and the top of his head, down his back, and all the way to the tip of his tail.

The male porcupine gives off his warning scent. Porcupines have a crescent of bare skin at the base of the back just above the tail. Special glands in this area give off a sharp odor that's uniquely porcupine.

But the cat doesn't pay attention to the porcupine's warnings. Mountain lions usually kill porcupines by knocking them out of trees. The fall often kills the porcupine. If it lives, it is very weak. The mountain lion can then climb down, flip the animal over onto its back, and bite its quill-free belly. This time, though, the male porcupine attacks first. He slams his tail into the mountain lion's shoulder. This drives the needle-sharp quills into the cat's flesh.

Hissing, the big cat quickly retreats down the tree and runs away. The mountain lion can't escape the quills, though. The tip of each quill has backward-pointing scales that work like hooks. When the mountain lion pulled away, the quills came out of the porcupine and stayed in the big cat's flesh. As the cat runs, each muscle movement drives the quills painfully deeper. Over the next few days, the irritating quills will travel deeper still. Several will eventually lodge against bones. Others will travel through muscle, pierce the skin, and be shed.

Neither the entry nor exit wounds will become infected. A porcupine's skin gives off a fatty substance that coats the quills' scales (*right*). This substance contains a chemical that kills bacteria (germs) that infect wounds. But the porcupine doesn't produce this chemical to protect its enemies. It does it to protect itself. Porcupines may accidentally quill themselves if they fall out of a tree, fight with another porcupine to defend their territory, or battle to earn a chance to mate.

The male porcupine peacefully spends his nights eating and his days sleeping. Then, one day, the male detects a special scent in the air. It's the scent of an adult female porcupine that is ready to mate. The male porcupine tracks this scent to the tree where the female is sleeping. When he starts to climb up to her, he discovers a rival male already in the tree. He screams an eerie high-pitched cry to challenge the other male. The rival screams back. The two males keep up this screaming match until they come face-to-face. Then they fight with bites and tail slaps. The rival male is younger and smaller and finally gives up. Each animal has quills sticking out of bloody cheeks and lips from their fight. The bigger male drives him out of the tree and wins the chance to mate.

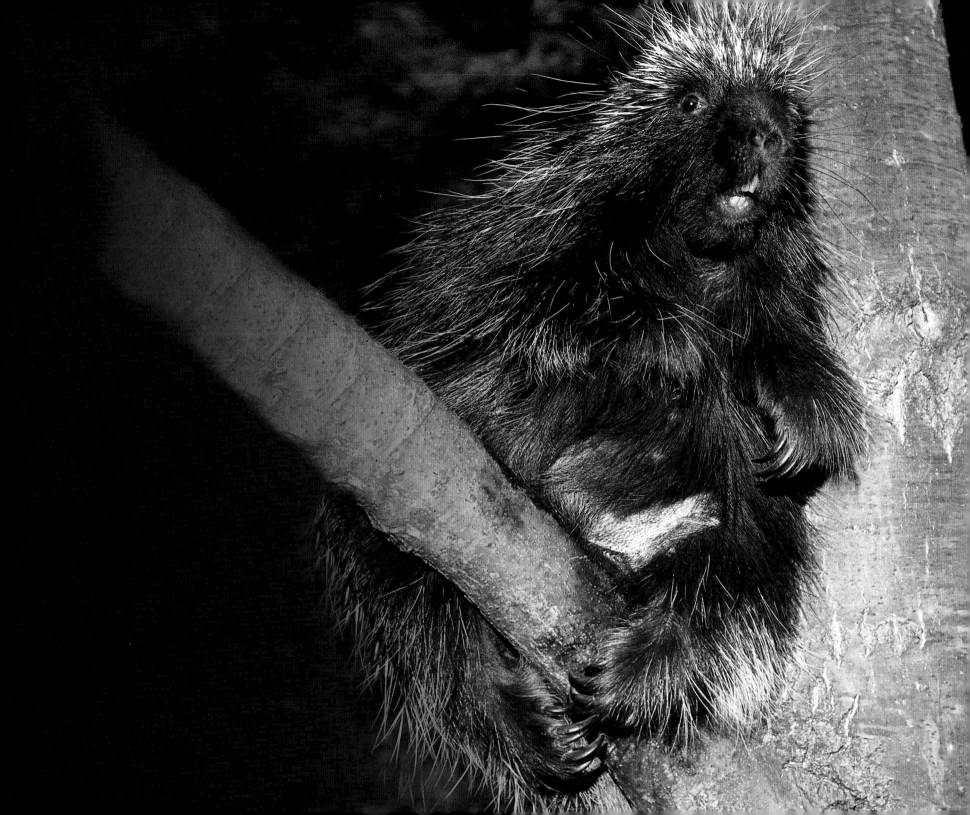

If he has the chance, the male porcupine will also mate with other females. But the nights are becoming longer and colder. So he spends more time eating. When a farmer's apple crop is ripe, the porcupine expands his territory to include the orchard. He feasts on apples as well as leaves. Occasionally, he also has a craving for salt. Porcupines need sodium, the chemical that is in salt, for their bodies to function properly.

Most plants have very little sodium. So the male porcupine seeks out foods that are high in sodium. These include water lilies and other aquatic (water) plants. The porcupine's quills are lightweight and spongy, like plastic foam. They buoy him up as he swims in search of a sodium-rich meal.

He doesn't find the plants he needs. Instead, the male porcupine returns to a source of salt he's visited before—a nearby cabin. Wood that has been handled by people soaks up the natural salt that is on their skin. The male porcupine climbs on an outdoor table. He uses his chisel-like teeth to scrape salty wood from the frame of a window that people often open with their hands.

Then one day, it snows. The male porcupine's woolly undercoat is like long underwear. It traps body heat close to his skin. This way, snow doesn't melt on his back. It builds up into a kind of overcoat that helps block the wind. He stays in the tree until icy wind gusts force him to climb down. Then he takes shelter in a den, a natural space in a rocky area.

A porcupine can't go for
more than a day or two
without eating. As soon
as the weather improves
a little, the male leaves
his den. His legs are so
short that his belly and tail
carve a channel in the snow. It takes
a lot of energy to travel through
the snow. So he goes to
a feeding tree that
is close by.

In the winter, when there are no leaves, porcupines eat bark. Birch trees have peeling outer bark, so the porcupine can more easily get at the inner bark—the part he eats. He uses his sharp teeth to pull away the outer bark. Then he scrapes off the tender inner bark.

One day, a mountain lion stalks and kills a deer in the part of the forest that is the male porcupine's home range.

By the time the male porcupine passes by, only some frozen bits of meat still cling to the bones. He isn't interested in the deer carcass—only curious. He doesn't realize that another animal, a fisher, is in a tree nearby.

The fisher is a scavenger, waiting to grab a meal of scraps from the carcass. When he spots the porcupine, he becomes a hunter and slips stealthily down the tree.

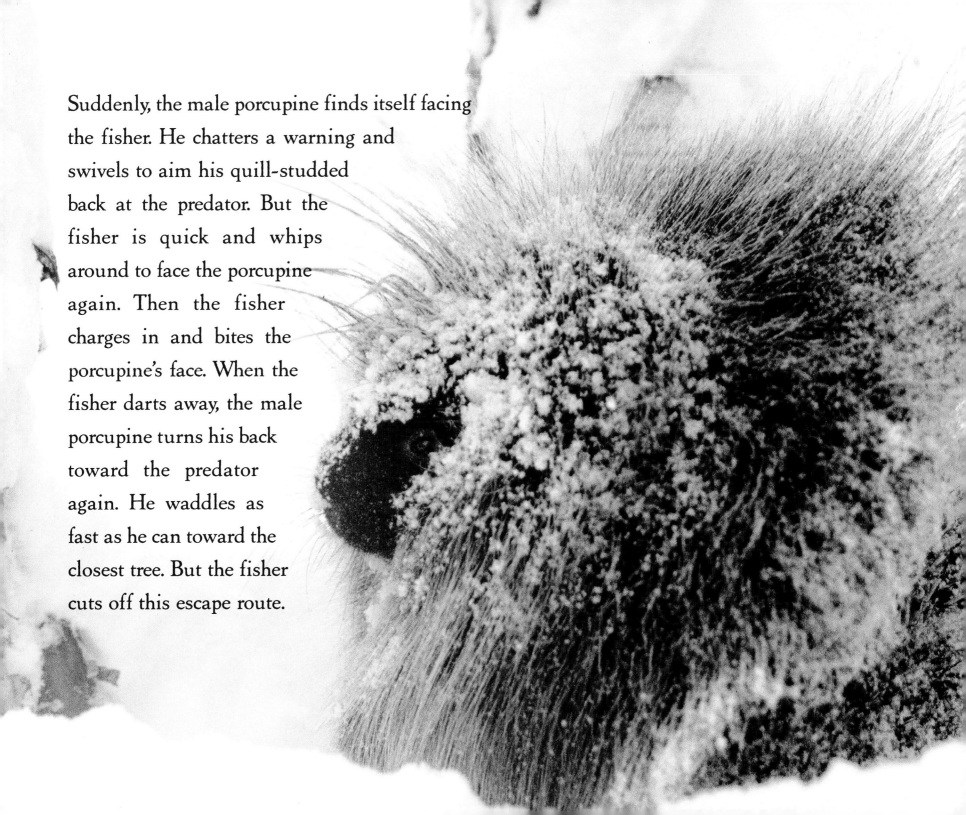

Suddenly, the male porcupine finds itself facing the fisher. He chatters a warning and swivels to aim his quill-studded back at the predator. But the fisher is quick and whips around to face the porcupine again. Then the fisher charges in and bites the porcupine's face. When the fisher darts away, the male porcupine turns his back toward the predator again. He waddles as fast as he can toward the closest tree. But the fisher cuts off this escape route.

The porcupine quickly turns away. Before the fisher can cut him off again, a noise catches the hunter's attention. This gives the male porcupine just enough time to squeeze into a hollow at the base of a nearby tree. The porcupine stays there with his quills aimed out and his vulnerable face and belly safely out of reach. Finally, the fisher gives up, eats its meal of scraps from the deer carcass, and leaves.

The male porcupine spends the rest of the winter searching for food and avoiding predators. By spring, the forest is full of delicious food choices once again. The porcupine's main focus is on eating his fill. Meanwhile, although he doesn't know it, the female he mated with gives birth to a little male.

Porcupines usually only have one baby at a time. The little baby male is about the size of a newborn puppy. He is born with his eyes open and with four front teeth. He also has a full coat of long hair to keep him warm. His tiny quills, soft at birth, harden in just a few hours. At birth, he is able to take care of himself. That's important because baby porcupines are left on their own on the ground. Their mothers climb down from their trees only when it's time to let them nurse.

It will be a few weeks before the youngster's short legs and claws grow long enough and strong enough for him to climb trees. So at first, he explores on the ground. He never wanders far from the tree where his mother is feeding.

When his mother comes down from the treetops, he hurries to her to nurse. After he finishes, she lingers to munch some leaves. He nibbles a little of her meal too before he falls asleep. This way, he begins to learn the smell and taste of the foods he'll soon need to find for himself.

One day, a fisher comes hunting while the female porcupine is on the ground with her youngster. She hurries onto a dead tree and turns to face the hunter. The fisher climbs another dead branch and watches for a chance to attack.

Meanwhile, the young male scurries to a nearby tree. He squeezes into a hole in the tree's trunk. His dark coloring helps keep him hidden. He stays in the tree until the fisher gives up and goes off to search for easier prey.

As soon as his nails are strong enough, the young male porcupine starts to climb. He will spend most of his time in the treetops near his mother. When he stops nursing, he'll begin moving onto branches— even trees—of his own choosing.

By October the young male is feeding alone. Within two years, he'll reach his adult size and expand his territory. When he's four, he'll be big and strong enough to fight a rival male and win an opportunity to mate. Then another generation of porcupines will join the cycle of life, the constant struggle between predators and prey.

Looking Back

- Take another look at the photo on page 9 to check out the porcupine's teeth. Their front teeth have an extra coating of enamel, an adaptation for gnawing wood. What color is this coating?

- Look closely at the porcupine on page 17. How is this porcupine making sure it doesn't fall out of the tree?

- Go back to page 29. Why do you think the porcupine worked hard to make sure its back rather than its face was toward its enemy? Not sure, revisit page 27. The porcupine's back is the part that's armed with quills.

Glossary

DEN: an animal's shelter

NURSE: the process of young sucking on its mother's teat to obtain milk

PREDATOR: an animal that hunts and eats other animals in order to survive

PREY: an animal that a predator catches to eat

QUILL: a stiff, hollow, protective spine

SCAVENGER: an animal that feeds on dead animals

TERRITORY: a home range that an animal defends against intruders

More Information

Books

Art, Henry W., and Michael W. Robbins. *Woodswalk: Peepers, Porcupines, and Exploding Puff Balls*. North Adams, MA: Storey Publishing, 2003. Investigate the porcupine's forest ecosystem, the animals that live there, and the way it changes with the seasons.

Green, Carl R., William R. Sanford Schroeder, and Baker Street Productions. *The Porcupine*. Parsippany, NJ: Crestwood House, 1985. This is an introduction to the porcupine's life cycle.

Sherrow, Victoria. *The Porcupine*. New York: Dillon Press, 1996. This book looks at the porcupine's physical features, habits, and its environment.

Websites

Native American Quillwork
http://www.native-languages.org/quillwork.htm
Find out how Native Americans traditionally have used porcupine quills to create works of art, decorate their clothes, and make jewelery. Follow links to find out how the quills are prepared and dyed using natural dyes.

What about Porcupines?
http://www.pnl.gov/pals/resource_cards/porcupines.stm
In addition to checking out facts about porcupines, explore activities and follow links to sites with additional information.

Index

With love, for Noah Daniel Beckdahl

The author would like to thank the following people for sharing their expertise and enthusiasm: Dr. Uldis Roze, Professor Emeritus, Biology Department, Queens College, New York, and author of *The North American Porcupine* (Smithsonian Press); Dr. Richard Sweitzer, Associate Professor, Wildlife and Conservation, University of North Dakota; and Dr. Dominique Berteaux, Canada Research Chair in Conservation of Northern Ecosystems, University of Quebec at Rimouski. The author would also like to express a special thank-you to Skip Jeffery for his help and support during the creative process.

Photo Acknowledgments

The images in this book are used with the permission of: © Michael Quinton/Minden Pictures, p. 1; © Tom and Pat Leeson/leesonphoto.com, p. 3; © Tim Jackson/Oxford Scientific Stock Images/Jupiterimages, p. 4; © Darrell Gulin/CORBIS, p. 5; © Chase Swift/CORBIS, p. 7; © Gerry Ellis/Minden Pictures, p. 9; © Daniel J. Cox/naturalexposures.com, pp. 10, 13, 24; © Dr. Uldis Roze, pp. 11, 17, 18, 31, 37; © Tom Brakefield/CORBIS, pp. 14, 26; © Dwight R. Kuhn, p. 15; © Eileen R. Herrling/ERH Photography, p. 19; © Tom Mangelson/naturepl.com, p. 20; © Lynn M. Stone/naturepl.com, p. 21; © Thomas Kitchin & Victoria Hurst, p. 22; © MARESA PRYOR/Animals Animals - Earth Scenes, p. 23; © D. Robert & Lorri Franz/CORBIS, pp. 25, 27, 33; © Kitchin & Hurst/leesonphoto.com, p. 29; © Robert E. Barber, p. 32; © Gerard Fuehrer/DRK PHOTO, pp. 34, 35; © Altrendo Nature by Getty Images, p. 36. Cover: © D. Robert & Lori Franz/CORBIS.

Lerner Publications Company
A division of Lerner Publishing Group
241 First Avenue North
Minneapolis, MN 55401 U.S.A.

Website address: www.lernerbooks.com

Library of Congress Cataloging-in-Publication Data

Markle, Sandra.
   Porcupines / by Sandra Markle.
     p.   cm. — (Animal prey)
   Includes bibliographical references and index.
   ISBN-13: 978-0-8225-6439-3 (lib. bdg. : alk. paper)
   ISBN-10: 0-8225-6439-4 (lib. bdg. : alk. paper)
   1. Porcupines—Juvenile literature. I. Title. II. Series: Markle, Sandra. Animal prey.
QL737.R652M37 2007
599.35'97—dc22
                                         2006000601

Manufactured in the United States of America
1 2 3 4 5 6 – DP – 12 11 10 09 08 07